CW01011180

Opening up
Hebrews

PHILIP H HACKING

DayOne

Opening up
Hebrews

PHILIP HACKING

'Hebrews is a difficult book for twenty-first century Christians to understand and relate to. In *Opening up Hebrews,* Philip Hacking outlines its meaning clearly and helpfully and relates its message to many issues that face us.

It is often not appreciated that the primary thrust of Hebrews is not intended to be doctrinal but pastoral and this handicaps our understanding and appreciation of the letter.

Philip's lengthy pastoral experience is invaluable in capturing and communicating this important aspect of

a much-neglected book and therefore
makes it accessible to those who are
keen to understand but daunted by the
obvious difficulties in getting to grips
with the text.'

Michael Plant
General Secretary of the Evangelical Fellowship of Congregational
Churches, Author of *Before the throne of God above—Jesus: our
heavenly High Priest*

ISBN 978-1-84625-042-2

9 781846 250422 >

British Library Cataloguing in Publication Data available

Published by Day One Publications
Ryelands Road, Leominster, HR6 8NZ
Telephone 01568 613 740   FAX 01568 611 473

email—sales@dayone.co.uk
web site—www.dayone.co.uk
North American—e-mail-sales@dayonebookstore.com
North American web site—www.dayonebookstore.com

Designed by Steve Devane and printed by Gutenberg Press, Malta

List of Bible abbreviations

THE OLD TESTAMENT		1 Chr.	1 Chronicles	Dan.	Daniel
		2 Chr.	2 Chronicles	Hosea	Hosea
Gen.	Genesis	Ezra	Ezra	Joel	Joel
Exod.	Exodus	Neh.	Nehemiah	Amos	Amos
Lev.	Leviticus	Esth.	Esther	Obad.	Obadiah
Num.	Numbers	Job	Job	Jonah	Jonah
Deut.	Deuteronomy	Ps.	Psalms	Micah	Micah
Josh.	Joshua	Prov.	Proverbs	Nahum	Nahum
Judg.	Judges	Eccles.	Ecclesiastes	Hab.	Habakkuk
Ruth	Ruth	S.of.S.	Song of Solomon	Zeph.	Zephaniah
1 Sam.	1 Samuel	Isa.	Isaiah	Hag.	Haggai
2 Sam.	2 Samuel	Jer.	Jeremiah	Zech.	Zechariah
1 Kings	1 Kings	Lam.	Lamentations	Mal.	Malachi
2 Kings	2 Kings	Ezek.	Ezekiel		

THE NEW TESTAMENT		Gal.	Galatians	Heb.	Hebrews
		Eph.	Ephesians	James	James
Matt.	Matthew	Phil.	Philippians	1 Peter	1 Peter
Mark	Mark	Col.	Colossians	2 Peter	2 Peter
Luke	Luke	1 Thes.	1 Thessalonians	1 John	1 John
John	John	2 Thes.	2 Thessalonians	2 John	2 John
Acts	Acts	1 Tim.	1 Timothy	3 John	3 John
Rom.	Romans	2 Tim.	2 Timothy	Jude	Jude
1 Cor.	1 Corinthians	Titus	Titus	Rev.	Revelation
2 Cor.	2 Corinthians	Philem.	Philemon		

Overview and background

We know very little about who wrote the book of
Hebrews—this is one of the great remaining mysteries of
the New Testament. Tradition had Paul in the frame, but the
style is wrong and the lack of personal greetings at the
beginning is probably conclusive, even though there is an
intriguing reference to his friend and colleague Timothy in
the closing chapter.

There have been many alternative suggestions, including
Barnabas and Apollos. Had Stephen lived longer he would
have been an ideal candidate, for the theme of the letter
follows beautifully from Acts 7 and the speech which led to
martyrdom. From a personal pronoun used in chapter 11
(v. 32), we do know that the writer was male, and the rest
must be wise conjecture.

Clearly the author must also have been a Jew, given his
knowledge of the temple ritual and his deep concern for
the Jewish nation. Hebrews was probably written before
AD 70, so the Jerusalem temple would still have been in
full use. The author is writing urgently to Hebrew Christians
scattered throughout the eastern world and in danger of
drifting away from their new-found faith in Jesus (2:1 and
10:39). In the Roman world the Jewish faith was
permitted; the Christian faith very often persecuted. It
would be only too easy to forsake the latter and go back to
the former.

9

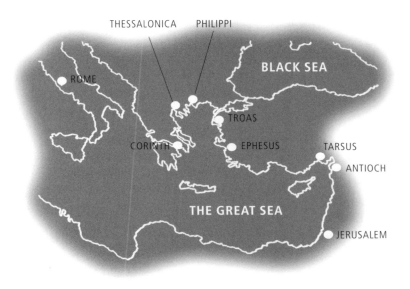

THESSALONICA   PHILIPPI

ROME

BLACK SEA

TROAS

CORINTH   EPHESUS

TARSUS

ANTIOCH

THE GREAT SEA

JERUSALEM

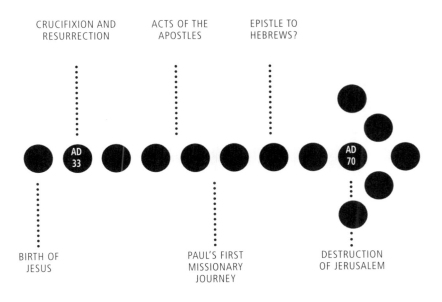

CRUCIFIXION AND RESURRECTION

ACTS OF THE APOSTLES

EPISTLE TO HEBREWS?

AD 33

AD 70

BIRTH OF JESUS

PAUL'S FIRST MISSIONARY JOURNEY

DESTRUCTION OF JERUSALEM

OPENING UP HEBREWS

The writer calls this document in 13:22 'only a short letter'. We in our terse e-mail age may disagree with the adjective (to read the letter aloud would take about an hour!). Nor does it seem too much like a letter with its deep theological teaching and lack of personal greetings. Yet the various solemn warnings about the dangers of falling away come from a very personal, pastoral heart.

So for the modern reader, the teaching about the uniqueness of Jesus Christ, his atoning work on the cross, and his glorious resurrection and ascension remains encouragingly true. It also comes with a relevant word of challenge to Christians in danger of compromise, not least in our multi-faith, post-modern, easily tolerant age. Like Paul in his letter to the Colossians, this unknown writer will meet prevalent false teaching with a bold proclamation that Jesus is 'superior' (1:4), and that word runs like a theme through the letter, occurring thirteen times. Opening up such a book will bring many surprises, both delightful and demanding. It will particularly challenge those of us who want a comfortable religious experience without the apparent intolerance of the Bible's insistence on the uniqueness of Jesus, Son of God. For our age, this letter speaks with remarkable, often uncomfortable, relevance.

1 Jesus, Son of God

(1:1-2:4)

Here, at the very beginning of this letter, we are taken straight to the point: a unique revelation leads in turn to a unique responsibility.

The finality of the message (1:1-2a)

Christians believe that God is a speaking God. The first chapter of the Bible is punctuated by the phrase 'and God said'. In the New Testament one of the great titles of Jesus is 'The Word'. Immediately we are crossing swords with much of modern liberal theology which ridicules the concept of a faith based on propositional statements. The recipients of this letter believed without doubt that God had spoken in the past. Only thus could mankind have any knowledge of what God is like.

The opening verse of Hebrews tells how God spoke in the past 'many times and in various ways'. God has spoken through the created world (Ps. 19). This is what Job calls God's 'whisper', 'the outer fringe of his works' (Job 26:14). A clearer view of God's character and demands is given as he speaks through law, prophets, poetry and history in the pages of the Old Testament.

There is always unfinished business in those Scriptures, so that we do not move from the less true to the more true when we pass Malachi; rather, we move from promise to fulfilment. In this letter we will see that worked out supremely in the themes of temple, priesthood, sacrifice and covenant. 'God had planned something better for us so that only together with us would they be made perfect' (11:40).

One of the common misconceptions of our day is the belief that the Old Testament is dominated by the theme of the judgement of God and the New Testament by that of the love of God. In fact, both themes run together in both Testaments and reach their highest fulfilment in the New. That fits with verse 2 and its reference to God speaking by his Son 'in these last days'. That phrase 'in these last days' is shorthand for the whole era of grace in which we live, between the first and second comings of Christ. All roads in the Bible lead to him and revelation is complete in him. Beyond him the church's task is to interpret these truths within the context of our day, but there is no further new revelation from God. He has spoken finally in Jesus Christ.

The supremacy of the messenger (1:2b-14)

Seven phrases are used in verses 2b-4 to undergird the claims of the uniqueness of Jesus, a challenge in those days and a stumbling block in our easy, tolerant age. He is the 'heir of all things', 'through whom [God] made the universe'; 'the radiance of God's glory'; 'the exact representation of his being', 'sustaining all things by his powerful word', who, after having 'provided purification for sins', 'sat down at the right hand of the Majesty in heaven.' He is seen as the author of creation, the theme of Proverbs 8:22-31, where he is 'Wisdom' personified (as with the 'Word' in John 1:1-3). Paul will pick up this message in Colossians 1:15-17, where Christ's creative ministry is enshrined in three memorable phrases—'by him … for him … in him'.

This perspective gives a new dimension to the Christmas story. So we sing 'Lo within a manger lies, he who built the starry skies',[1] or 'Hands that flung stars into space to cruel nails surrendered',[2] as we link Christmas with Easter.

The thought of Jesus as sovereign over the universe puts international terror and personal problems into a right perspective, particularly when we are reminded of his unique activity in the drama of cross, resurrection and ascension (v. 3b). This is no theological nit-picking. Jesus, seated at God's right hand with victory accomplished, is central to our assurance of salvation and should be reflected in our songs of praise and in the balance of our liturgy, especially around the Lord's Table. For these truths the Reformers died. Let us not betray them by our mindless compromise.

> The thought of Jesus as sovereign over the universe puts international terror and personal problems into a right perspective, particularly when we are reminded of his unique activity in the drama of cross, resurrection and ascension.

> If Jesus is Son of God and God's last word, how unthinkable it is to ignore his message, and how dangerous to think of turning back from him!

The 'right hand' of God speaks of the place of authority which belongs to Jesus by right as God's Son. Significantly, he is now there as our high priest, one of the great themes of this letter. This was red-hot teaching for Jewish Christians, with temple worship still proceeding; it should be a powerful reminder to us not to go back to Old Testament ritual. There was a great cost for Jesus in that ministry (5:8-10), so its fruit should never be taken lightly.

We are then taken on a tour of seven Old Testament passages, largely from the Psalms, to assure the first readers of Christ's superiority over angels. This may not be a burning issue for our day, but with the proliferation of alternative spiritualities, often quite pagan and yet with Christian overtones, we do need to listen. The repeated theme is the uniqueness of sonship, and the humbler role of angelic ministry.

The first chapter closes with two quotations so relevant to our twenty-first century world. Perhaps we, more than any previous generation, know that this planet has a sell-by date. What Christians can offer to our environmentally-obsessed society is the truth that God in Christ has the last word and that, using the oft-repeated quote from Psalm 110 (1:13), the Jesus we worship is already in the place of power over history. Such a dynamic truth brings great comfort, but also an awesome responsibility.

The demands of the gospel (2:1-4)

This is a practical letter which pulls no punches and 2:1-4 is the first of five solemn warnings not to be glossed over (compare with 3:7-19; 5:11-14; 6:1-8; 10:26-31). Already the writer is reminding his Jewish readers of the danger of drifting away. They knew how authoritative was the Old Testament law sealed at Sinai; now they must be warned how much more demanding is the gospel of salvation: 'For if the message spoken by angels was binding, and every violation and disobedience received its just punishment, how shall we escape if we ignore such a great salvation?' (vv. 2-3).

If Jesus is Son of God and God's last word, how unthinkable it is to ignore his message, and how dangerous to think of turning back from him! The message had come with absolute clarity from eye-witnesses and with unique signs and wonders to match and reinforce it. To accept Jesus will often be very costly; to reject him will always be more costly and very foolish, for where else can we go (see John 6:68-69)?

For further study ▶

FOR FURTHER STUDY

1. Read Colossians 1:15-17. What is the significance of the phrases 'by him ... for him ... in him'?

2. Study the passages of warning (2:1-4; 3:7-19; 5:11-14; 6:1-8; 10:26-31). Why have these warnings been given to us?

TO THINK ABOUT AND DISCUSS

1. Why is it so important to have a right understanding of who Jesus is and what he has done?

2. How should we respond to times of international fear and insecurity, given that we know Jesus is sovereign over the whole universe? What difference should this knowledge make to the whole of our lives—to our values, perspectives and choices?

3. What attitude should Christians have towards environmental concerns? Should we care about pollution or global warming if Jesus is in control of all things? Justify your response from the Bible.

2 Jesus, only Saviour

(2:5-18)

The unique wonder of the Christian gospel is that the Son of God became a man LIKE us, in total humanity, in order that he might become the man FOR us.

A man like us

There will always be mysteries about the humanity of Jesus when we think of his essential deity. How did he grow up? What were the sphere and reality of his temptations? Were there self-imposed limits to his knowledge? What is certain is contained in verse 17. He was like us 'in every way'. That includes his maleness, so that we cannot in a misplaced inclusive zeal say that he was like his brothers and sisters in every way; he did not share his sisters' femininity.

The writer quotes from Psalm 8, which had proclaimed the uniqueness of mankind in the created order: we were made 'in the image of God' (Gen. 1:27) with authority over creation under God himself, and with God-given ability to make choices, leading both to great evil and remarkable goodness. In the words of Pascal, the French philosopher, mankind is 'the glory and scum of the universe'. Yet man was made 'a little lower than the angels' and has been given authority over the world to come (v. 5). That is a great statement of faith, given the evidence of man's frailty and disobedience in this present world. For Jesus, the glory and honour were his rights; the humanity, a willing lowly descent.

We cannot doubt therefore that Jesus shared our temptations to the full: 'He himself suffered when he was tempted' (v. 18). This truth is repeated in 4:15, to emphasize it. He also was able not to sin. We dare not subtly change that phrase and suggest that he was not able to sin, as we would then destroy the reality of his humanity. Indeed, his temptations went way beyond what we can know, we who so often fall at the first or second hurdle in temptation's pathway.

All of this was to enable Jesus to be our representative in the great plan of salvation. He had to 'taste death for everyone' (v. 9). In his manhood and mortality he shared our lot so that in his ministry he might become our 'Pathfinder'. The word translated 'author' in verse 10 is very rich biblically. It is given as 'Prince' in Acts 5:31, but 'author' here, in 12:2 and Acts 3:15. The word speaks of one who goes before to open up the way. In military terms it includes the note of risk and sacrifice. In the Old Testament narrative it has a parallel in the Joseph story, when a betrayed brother came through rejection and prison to be a prince and a saviour of his own family, even of those who had been the agents of his suffering. Joseph sums it up thus in Gen 50:20—'You intended to harm me, but God intended it for good to accomplish ... the saving of many lives.'

In his remarkable representative ministry, Jesus had to know the discipline mentioned in verse 10, enough to boggle any mind, that of being made 'perfect through suffering'. How the Son of God could be made perfect is incredible and humbling. It means that we have a fully sympathetic Saviour, one who is 'able to help those who are being tempted' (v. 18); an example to us in the hour of testing, but also a unique person, seen supremely in the cross which is ever central in this letter and the whole of the Christian faith.

The man for us

This title is the meaningful description of Christ given by the German theologian Dietrich Bonhoeffer, who suffered much for his faith. The three great Christian festivals help us to keep the balance here: Christmas speaks of God WITH us; Easter, of God FOR us; Pentecost, of God IN us. Beware of any sub-Christian message which wants the first and last without the middle. Then you would have an empty sandwich of an incarnational witness to the world without a saving message to the sinner, or an experiential offer without an atoning substance. The cross is always the centre, and constantly the scandal.

For Jesus there could be no shortcut. Verse 9 reminds us that he could only be crowned with glory because first 'he suffered death' on our behalf. So his great temptations, both in the wilderness at the start of his ministry (see Matt. 4:1-11) and in the garden at the end (Luke 22:39-46) were aimed to cause him to bypass the cross. Thankfully he defeated Satan and we can rejoice in the truths of verses 14-15. The verb 'destroy' speaks of taking the deadly fuse out of a killer bomb. Brave men still risk and often lose their lives doing that dangerous work to save others. For them it is high risk; for Jesus a dead certainty, but with resurrection to follow for him and untold blessings to us.

The whole purpose behind the coming of Jesus into the world was that he might destroy the works of the devil (compare 1 John 3:8 with v. 14). Thus in countless churches across the globe people enter on Christmas Day to celebrate the birth of Jesus by eating bread and drinking wine to commemorate his death. That really is as unique as Jesus himself is unique.

For his Jewish readers, the writer now begins to move into the central thesis of his letter, using the analogy of the Day of Atonement, so central to Old Testament worship.

There the high priest, on behalf of his people, entered into the holiest place in the Temple covered with the sacrificial blood of animals. The solemn ritual had to be repeated year after year, since the ritual was only symbolic, waiting for that great day when the final, once-for-all sacrifice would have been made and the way to God made possible for all. History was turned on its head that day outside Jerusalem's walls when Jesus, the God-man, cried triumphantly 'It is finished', and the temple curtain was torn from top to bottom, the work of God's hand not man's revolution. How dare we ever go back behind that truth!

FOR FURTHER STUDY

1. Consider the title of 'Pathfinder' given to Jesus. What are its implications for our faith?

2. What are the different emphases in Christian truth we convey when we call Jesus: 'man'; 'a man'; 'the man'?

TO THINK ABOUT AND DISCUSS

1. How does it encourage us to know that Jesus is a man like us, who lived and walked on this earth, and was tempted just as we are? How does it encourage us also to know that he is so much more than just a man?

2. In what ways are we sometimes tempted to deny the truth of what Christ has done for us?

3 The true promise

(3:1-4:13)

Great truths have great implications. The favourite link word 'therefore' (v. 1) takes us onwards as it takes us back to some great Old Testament passages now gloriously fulfilled in Jesus.

These verses are like some geological strata or rings on an ancient tree as, through Christian eyes, we look at Moses, Joshua and David, and discover that all are pointing to one greater than they, and that even the land of promise is pointing forwards. In the process we discover that we are utterly dependent on the truth and power of scripture.

Look to the Lord (3:1-6)

To the Jew, Moses stands supreme as the pioneer leader of the nation; to the Jewish Christian respect for Moses continues, but 'Jesus has been found worthy of greater honour than Moses'—such is the testimony of verse 3. That follows from the truth of the next verses, which depict Jesus as equal with God, as the builder of the house, and Moses as a distinguished servant and happy to be no other.

As the writer is urging his readers to persevere to the end he uses the faithfulness of Jesus as the key inspiration (v. 6). It is a valuable exercise deliberately to keep our gaze on the Jesus of the Gospels. He had a unique life and work but we too have a heavenly calling (v. 1), and as he was sent into the world as 'apostle and high priest' (v. 1), so we too are sent (compare John 20:21) and need to keep looking in the right direction for inspiration. The powerful incentive for the Christian servant is to remember that the unique Son became a willing servant in fulfilling his earthly ministry (Mark 10:45). In that remarkable drama of Jesus washing his rebellious disciples' feet, the real punchline is John 13: 13-14: 'You call me "Teacher" and "Lord", and rightly so, for that is what I am. Now that I, your Lord and Teacher, have washed your feet, you also should wash one another's feet.' He is claiming his rightful position as Master and Lord, even when doing the job of a slave, thus abolishing all status-seeking in the kingdom of God and transforming the whole concept of service.

Look to the Word (3:7-4:19)

This writer would have had little sympathy for the modern habit of keeping scripture portions to the minimum in our worship services and he would be overjoyed in churches where the rustling of pages signifies a congregation following the preacher's exposition. He might have been challenged by the use of data projectors to display scripture passages, making the personal bible redundant! All his teaching in this argument about promise and fulfilment is punctuated by Old Testament quotations and a complete confidence in the authority of Scripture. Words of the psalmist are cited as the work of the Holy Spirit (3:7) and the voice of God (4:3), even while still recognizing them as the writing of David (4:7).

This passage contains a word of promise. There was only a tiny remnant of the exodus people who reached the Promised Land, but the promise remains of a greater fulfilment in this wonderful tapestry of Scripture: 'There remains, then, a Sabbath-rest for the people of God' (4:9). All down the centuries Christian saints have found comfort here, not only in the hope of the final heavenly rest, but already in the rest that comes from trust in Jesus and all he has done for us. It is all there in the well-known offer of Matthew 11:28-30: 'Come to me, all you who are weary and burdened, and I will give you rest. Take my yoke upon you and learn from me, for I am gentle and humble in heart, and you will find rest for your souls. For my yoke is easy and my burden is light.'

A preacher often discovers the wrong people listening to his sermons. When he challenges to action, the already fully committed fasten their belts more tightly for take-off; when he offers rest in the Lord, the half asleep go fully asleep. So here the promised rest is hedged around by many warnings. The Israelites in the wilderness had known forty years of aimless wandering because of rebellion (3:16), sin (3:17), disobedience (3:18) and unbelief (3:19). All these characteristics of fallen men and women are still with us—hence these words of warning.

The long quote from Psalm 95 in 3:7-11 used to be part of the regular diet of Anglican worship in the age of the Book of Common Prayer. It meant that every Sunday morning, worshippers were solemnly reminded of the danger of missing out on God's glorious promises. Somehow our modern worship prefers the lighter touch! It may also be significant that these verses include a threefold repetition of the word 'today', giving extra urgency to the whole theme. Most of us prefer to put off challenges until tomorrow, which has a habit of never coming.

Both the word of promise and the word of warning come with a word of power. There is something awesome about the picture in 4:12-13. The actual anatomical detail of 'soul and spirit, joints and marrow' may be hard to define, but the reminder of a two-edged sword is clear enough. We may use the sword of the Spirit to bring new life into many situations (Eph. 6:17), but first we must open ourselves to its

> We may use the sword of the Spirit to bring new life into many situations but first we must open ourselves to its dynamic influence in our own lives. As one day we will stand uncovered before God our Judge, so now we must dare to be open before God's Word, letting it be a hammer to drive home necessary truths (Jer. 23:29) or a mirror to show us our sorry state before we begin putting things right (James 1:22-25).

dynamic influence in our own lives. As one day we will stand uncovered before God our Judge, so now we must dare to be open before God's Word, letting it be a hammer to drive home necessary truths (Jer. 23:29) or a mirror to show us our sorry state before we begin putting things right (James 1:22-25).

Look to yourselves (4:1-13)

The story of the wilderness, which Paul also expounds in 1 Corinthians 10, was very relevant to these Hebrew Christians. Some even suggest that the term 'forty years' would have rung a bell, signifying the gap between the days of Jesus and the date of writing this letter. What is certain is that the twin dangers faced by the Israelites in the exodus period were still a temptation then, and are still a temptation today: there must be no turning back, and no stopping short.

With short memories, the Israelites quickly forgot both the misery of slavery in Egypt and the wonderful miracle of the Red Sea, and plotted to go back. The 'sinful, unbelieving heart' of 3:12 will always move men and women, however well instructed, away from the living God. In a similar way, Stephen spoke in his powerful sermon recorded in Acts 7 of the Israelites who 'in their hearts turned back to Egypt' (7:39). There are two antidotes to this heart problem. One is a regular spiritual health check—'see to it, brothers' (3:12)—and the other is a mutual encouragement which can only come within a loving, honest, church fellowship (3:13).

As a boy I always preferred the short sprints in the school athletics. The pain was soon over. The Christian life, however, is a marathon race, and, just as the vast majority in the wilderness never reached the goal, so these Hebrew Christians under pressure were in danger of falling short (4:1). Whether interpreted as the final rest of heaven or the peace of godly assurance, the message is clear enough, and this letter is punctuated by warnings to challenge complacency (e.g. in 2:1). The final exhortation of this passage sums it up: 'Let us, therefore, make every effort to enter that rest, so that no one will fall by following their example of disobedience' (4:11). In a semi-paradox, we are called to 'make every effort' to enter 'rest'.

The best way to keep stable in the Christian life, now as then, is to be balanced. We must learn to trust God's promises and not imagine we can earn our salvation by sheer determination. On the other hand, we must be deaf to those siren voices telling us to sit back and leave it all to God. Nobody 'can be carried to the skies on flowery beds of ease'.

For further study ▶

FOR FURTHER STUDY

1. Study Psalm 95. What are the different themes contained in this psalm, and how do they encourage us to worship God?
2. Think through the Bible's verdict on its own authority, with special reference to 2 Timothy 3:16 and 2 Peter 1:21.

TO THINK ABOUT AND DISCUSS

1. In what ways can 'status-seeking' be seen in churches? How can we follow Jesus' example of being a servant to our brothers and sisters?
2. In what ways are we tempted to 'turn back' or 'fall short'? How, practically, do we 'make every effort to enter that rest'? How can we encourage one another to persevere in this?
3. What are the specific temptations you experience which keep you from pursuing this goal?

4 The true priest

(4:14-5:14)

In church history, the word 'priest' has often been at the centre of controversy. The New Testament never uses the word with reference to ministers within the church, giving the title to Christ alone. This was a revolution in itself, with all the Jewish history of priesthood.

B ut the once-for-all sacrifice of Calvary decisively ended the Jewish priesthood, demonstrating that now no more priests or animal sacrifices are required. It is a pity that in the rubrics of the 1662 Book of Common Prayer the word 'priest' was kept as an Anglicization of the Greek 'presbuteros'. Much confusion would have been saved, and the ways of church history changed, if they had simply translated it as 'presbyter'.

With the Reformation there was a rediscovery of the 'priesthood of all believers', echoing Peter's bold assertion in 1 Peter 2:9—'you are a chosen people, a royal priesthood'. The church IS, not HAS, a priesthood, but we do have a unique high priest now at God's right hand, bringing confidence and challenge to his people.

A truth to encourage you (4:14-16)

The Christian faith is built on the facts of history—hence the stress in early apostolic preaching on the resurrection of Jesus, including the facts of the empty tomb and the long list of witnesses to his appearances (see 1 Cor. 15:5-8). This letter majors on the subsequent truth of the ascended Lord 'who has gone through the heavens' (4:14). Yet the exalted Lord remains the Jesus of history, of the cradle, the carpenter's shop and the cross. So he can fully sympathize with our humanity, even with our frailty.

> The Gospels remind us of the reality of the testings of Jesus throughout his life, brought to a climax in Gethsemane, 'yet [he] was without sin' (5:15). He supremely stood firm, at great cost, and stands with us now in our testing moments.

Sometimes we assume that those who have fallen into a particular sin are best able to understand and help others, after repentance, of course. But Scripture suggests that those who have known the full force of a particular temptation and yet stood firm are the best counsellors, if they retain the humility which comes from grace. The Gospels remind us of the reality of the testings of Jesus throughout his life, brought to a climax in Gethsemane, 'yet [he] was without sin' (4:15). He supremely stood firm, at great cost, and stands with us now in our testing moments. It may well be significant that the High Priest, always seated in heaven, is only seen once as standing, and that is in Acts 7:56 as Stephen goes to his Christlike martyrdom.

These facts should stimulate our faith. So in these verses, the writer brings a double exhortation. He calls us to 'hold firmly to the faith we profess', and then challenges us to a new spirit of boldness (4:16). Christians are called to be bold in their witness to others (e.g. 10:23) but here and elsewhere (e.g. 10:19) this boldness is to be seen in the spirit of prayer. We can come to 'the throne of grace' (4:16) because of Christ's death and resurrection. Sometimes the reluctance to pray and the timidity of our requests for ourselves and others suggests a lack of gratitude for this access into God's presence. We may be critical of the formality and deadness of prayers in other religions. Yet all too often their devotees put us to shame in their dedication and regularity.

A truth to enrich you (5:1-10)

Selecting people for the ordained ministry is quite a delicate task. You have to look for two parallel realities—a sense of divine calling and some evidence of a character that demonstrates sympathy with people and confidence in the truth of God's Word. It was not altogether different in the better days of Old Testament history, with the extra qualification of coming from the right tribe. Mercifully, that last element has now been removed from the equation in the Christian ministry. Equally, our ministry today does not involve animal sacrifices and the ritual of the day of Atonement, since

Calvary has fulfilled and therefore abolished both.

The first readers of this letter knew well the truths of
5:1-4. The priest was himself a sinner ('he himself is subject
to weakness', v. 2) and therefore needed to offer sacrifices for
himself first, and yet he had to be aware of the dignity of a
heavenly calling demanding consistency of life. History
records that, sadly, this was often not the case with the priests
chosen—seen most grimly at the time of the trial and
crucifixion of Jesus.

Jesus himself had no priestly pedigree and yet he certainly
knew the divine appointment to his unique high priesthood.
The writer to the Hebrews quotes two very significant
psalms to prove his point and gently introduces the character
of Melchizedek, a shadowy Old Testament character of
remarkable importance whom we will meet again later. As
for Christ's human qualities to prove his fitness for this office,
verses 7-8 powerfully, almost startlingly, prove the case.

In these verses we are standing on holy ground, reminded
of the tears like drops of blood in Gethsemane as Jesus faced
the ultimate challenge of separation from his heavenly
Father, taking our place and offering the ultimate sacrifice.
Films can vividly portray the physical agony of the cross,
where the Bible account is strangely silent, but none can act
out the deep spiritual torment of it all. An old Sankey hymn
captures it:

> None of the ransomed ever knew
> how deep were the waters crossed;
> nor how dark was the night that the Lord passed through
> ere he found his sheep that was lost.[3]

Here truth is pushed to the extremes of credulity as we read that 'although he was a son, he learned obedience from what he suffered' (v. 8). This willingly obedient substitute sacrifice becomes also the unique high priest representing us in heaven. Little wonder is it that this writer wants to plead with his readers, in danger of a cowardly return to the 'security' of the old days, to think again. In the climate of today, the same temptation to opt for a quiet life when faced with a philosophy which hates above all things the assumed intolerance of any dogmatic truth must be resisted, even if it means taking up a tiny cross on behalf of our suffering Saviour.

A truth to extend you (5:11-14)

Now comes the call to engage the mind. The Christian faith is not an intellectual exercise, but it is intellectually satisfying when we dare to think it through. However, immaturity is not just for the mentally lazy, since often the intellect is not over-ready to entertain any idea that the heart finds unpalatable. I have spent most of my ministry in areas populated by people of high academic ability. Two things I have consistently observed: in the first place, many gifted people are extremely and rightly humble in matters of faith, but equally there are those who hide a personal moral problem behind a cloak of intellectual argument.

So the writer brings his gentle but firm rebuke about immaturity (5:11-14). He sees his readers as still being babies needing milk, when they should have been enjoying solid food and even teaching others. This has shades of Paul, who has similar complaints in 1 Corinthians 3:1-3: 'Brothers, I could not address you as spiritual but as worldly—mere infants in Christ. I gave you milk, not solid food, for you were not yet ready for it. Indeed, you are still not ready. You are still worldly. For since there is jealousy and quarrelling among you, are you not worldly?' There has always been a fatal misunderstanding about the Christian faith. It is true that we begin our pilgrimage as new-born babes needing the ABC of truth (1 Peter 2:2) and we remain ever childlike in our trust. However, CHILDLIKENESS is very different from CHILDISHNESS. No Christian is meant to be a perpetual Peter Pan. Beware of the temptation to join every Basics course that you can find.

The marks of maturity are not found in an encyclopaedic knowledge of the Bible, nor even a full grasp of the significance of our shadowy friend Melchizedek, waiting in the wings. Rather, they are seen in an ability to make moral judgements and not to be caught up in the childish wranglings and jealousies of the world. Baby Christians are in constant danger from a devil who delights to distract the people of God (see Eph. 4:14). So let God through his Word and Spirit help us to grow up. The world in this century, as in the first, needs to be confronted by a strong, mature church.

FOR FURTHER STUDY

1. Why does it matter that we recognize the New Testament meaning of the word 'priest'?

2. Boldness is a dominant characteristic in the New Testament. How does it affect our work and witness?

TO THINK ABOUT AND DISCUSS

1. What does it mean in practice to 'approach the throne of grace with confidence'? How can we ensure that our boldness is not presumption?

2. In what ways are we tempted to 'opt for a quiet life' today, e.g. in our witness to friends and family, or in our churches? How does Christ's example challenge us?

3. In what ways can we still behave like spiritual babies? What steps can we take to help ourselves and others to grow up to be mature 'adults'?

5 No turning back

(6:1-20)

Scripture is always honest, and sometimes brutally so. This is because eternal issues are at stake: it is not kind to gloss over problems or minimize dangers.

This letter also brings regular warnings, but always in the context of love. Here, in 6:9, the writer has a sudden burst of affection, with the only 'beloved' (NKJV) or 'dear friends' of the letter, aware perhaps of the solemnity of the previous verses. Love is never softness or compromise, but it is also never harsh or rude. 1 Corinthians 13 says it all.

The careful balance of this sixth chapter mirrors the balance of Scripture itself. The overall thrust is that of the security of the elect because our salvation depends not on merit or effort, but on the grace of God and the finished work of Christ on the cross. Yet here, as throughout the Bible, there are the occasional reminders of the possibility of falling away, and even of apostasy, so that that assurance does not degenerate into complacency. So Jesus can speak of the fate of Judas in the warning of John 15:2, 6. In a similar way, Paul speaks of his own spiritual discipline 'so that after I have preached to others, I myself will not be disqualified for the prize' (1 Cor. 9:27).

Take warning (6:1-8)

Standing still is a sure recipe for falling back. So in verse 1 we are encouraged to go on a journey, 'on to maturity'. The writer promises to accompany us. We help by getting alongside not shouting directions from a distance. There are six basic truths in these opening words of chapter 6. They are a somewhat formidable foundation course by our modern standards, but there will be no good building without them.

Significantly, this ABC begins with sin and repentance, in true New Testament fashion. Always beware if this is missing. In the same mode, resurrection hope and judgement go hand-in-hand with ways of initiation (baptism and laying-on of hands). Our twenty-first century churches would be much stronger if all our members had been well instructed in this way. Then there would be a springboard for exciting growth.

Yet even the best start does not make progress inevitable (see Gal. 5:7). Indeed, occasionally a professing Christian of good standing seems to deny his or her faith and join the enemy. Verses 4-8 make solemn reading, even though the writer immediately in the next verse expresses confidence that the warning signals will be heeded: 'Even though we speak like this, dear friends, we are confident of better things in your case—things that accompany salvation.' This is not a case of a sad period of backsliding, not uncommon in many

> As a non-gardener, I always treat horticultural analogies in Scripture with great deference, but even I can see the power of verses 7-8 and the contrast between the productive field and that which is clogged with thorns and thistles. Fields do not get like that overnight. We need to watch the lazy spirit which does not bother to notice how fast the weeds are growing and will not bend the back to do something about it.

Christians, but rather of a complete denial of the faith, with that terrible picture of 'crucifying the Son of God all over again' (v. 6). To reject the message of the cross, the authority of the Word of God, and the power of the Holy Spirit, is to put oneself outside the realm where God is at work. No sensible person plays with fire like that.

As a non-gardener, I always treat horticultural analogies in Scripture with great deference, but even I can see the power of verses 7-8 and the contrast between the productive field and that which is clogged with thorns and thistles. Fields do not get like that overnight. We need to watch the lazy spirit which does not bother to notice how fast the weeds are growing and will not bend the back to do something about it.

Take heart (6:9-12)

Confidence in self or others is a variable commodity, often completely dominated by feelings and wishful thinking. The writer here bases his confidence on the past record of these Hebrew Christians. Faith is always evidenced in works, and practical love was high on their CV, which gives him confidence for the future. In our attitude to others we can be unfair and very forgetful. God is neither (v. 10). So there is hope.

Still, it is vital to blend optimism with realism. Too many of us start well but never finish. The UK is littered with intriguing follies, where people started to build but never completed the task for various reasons, and church life has its own kind. My wife and I recently visited one of these architectural follies when on holiday. The builder even left his ladders against the wall of the unfinished building decades ago. The story of why he suddenly left makes fascinating reading. But spiritual follies are only tragedies. So verses 11-12 were vital and urgent reading for these readers—and for us now, too. In a similar spirit, on the vexed issue of Christian giving, Paul had to tell his Corinthian friends to make sure that their completion of the task matched their enthusiastic start: 'Now finish the work, so that your eager willingness to do it may be matched by your completion of it' (2 Cor. 8:11). The old adage is still true that 'the road to hell is paved with good intentions.'

Take hold (6:13-20)

For the subtle tendency to slip back under pressure, there are two great truths to grasp for a remedy. In the first place there is the promise of God and, to illustrate this truth, the writer goes back to Abraham, the great father of the Jewish nation, but, even more, the supreme example of one who took God at his word (v. 13-15). Abraham's faith in the assurance of a family, through whom God would bless the world, was sorely tested, but he kept believing because God had promised and he would never let him down. The principle remains the same except that these readers, and we today, have so much more to encourage faith.

What Abraham could only see dimly in the future has now become a reality, and here is the second great truth, called a hope and an anchor in 6:19. The metaphor is gloriously mixed, with the nautical reference becoming ecclesiastical— an anchor in the sanctuary! The surprise should alert us to the unexpected and dramatic. Not only do we have the promise of God, but also we have the very presence of Christ to strengthen us. That presence is Jesus in his high priestly role in heaven itself (v. 20), way beyond the wonder of the Jewish high priest and his annual appearance in the earthly sanctuary. There should be no turning back from that unique truth, and to challenge his readers further, the writer now draws on sacred history, bringing forward as his witness the shadowy but vital figure of Melchizedek.

FOR FURTHER STUDY

1. Consider the balance of Scripture in its warnings that we need not just a good foundation, but also to build well on it (see 1 Cor. 3:10-15).

2. Think about how warnings and encouragement often go hand in hand in the Bible. What is the relationship between the warnings and encouragements in the words of Jesus in John 15:1-18?

TO THINK ABOUT AND DISCUSS

1. How can we encourage one another to persevere to the end?

2. What kind of relationships do we need in our churches if we are to be able to tell if our brothers and sisters are falling away? How can we practically get alongside one another so that we will be able to give help and encouragement when needed, but without becoming interfering?

3. Have there been times when we have been tempted to doubt God's Word and his promises? How can we use God's Word to counteract our doubts in times of difficulty?

6 A voice from the past

(7:1-28)

Melchizedek has been waiting in the wings for some time; now in chapter 7 he takes centre stage, but only as a remarkable shadow of a very remarkable Saviour.

This king and high priest is a supreme example of the inspiration of Scripture. He only appears in a few verses in Genesis 14 (vv. 18-20), has a passing but important reference in Psalm 110:4, and then awaits his New Testament reinstatement. We can only assume that Melchizedek had his place in the Emmaus Road sermon of Jesus, when he explained how the things concerning himself were 'in all the Scriptures' (Luke 24:27).

In verse 3 the writer can claim that this Melchizedek was 'like the Son of God', as the shadow is cast from the reality. All the Old Testament types point forward to the unique reality of Jesus. So it was with this shadowy figure.

A remarkable shadow (7:1-10)

Much is read into the story of Genesis 14 and, with divine

inspiration, we may even read from the silence. Melchizedek appears and disappears, and we have no knowledge of his antecedents nor his successors, unlike the Jewish high priests whose office depended on their family tree. Dates of birth and death are not known. So he becomes one who, in that sense, has no beginning or end (v. 3).

There is, however, an intriguing silence in the writer to the Hebrews' interpretation of the Genesis narrative. In Genesis 14:18 Melchizedek brought out bread and wine to Abraham. Yet the author of Hebrews draws no sacramental parallel. Many modern theologians would have majored on this, a reminder of how far we often stray from the New Testament emphasis.

Here this remarkable Old Testament event presents an unusual man and an unusual moment. Melchizedek is unique as a king and a priest. These two roles could never be united, probably wise even in our twenty-first century. The stories of impatient King Saul (1 Samuel 13:7-15) and arrogant King Uzziah (2 Chronicles 26:16-21), both of whom tried to ignore the distinction between the roles, are recorded in the Bible as a warning. Yet here is an anticipation of the kingly high priesthood of Jesus Christ, always seen as seated in heaven, a regal position, not standing as a priest offering sacrifice. Perhaps we should see a strange prophetic note in the fact that the only crown ever worn by Jesus was the crown of thorns on his crucifixion day, and the only regal inscription given to him was over his cross.

There is more. Melchizedek's name speaks of righteousness and his title speaks of peace (v. 2). There is accuracy in the reference to 'God Most High' (v. 1), a strong pagan name for the Almighty. This strange priest was not in God's direct line, and yet Salem his home was the origin of Jerusalem. There is so much that is intriguing here. The main theme, however, is the anticipation of Jesus, whose death as the righteous sacrifice would alone bring peace with God (Rom. 5:1). All the Bible references to the relationship between righteousness and peace find their fulfilment in Christ (Ps. 85:10; Isa. 32:17; James 3:17-18).

> This unique promise of a priesthood that lasts for ever was necessary because then, as now, all religious ceremonies were imperfect and passing. The Old Testament law was always pointing forward to a day of fulfilment, not to a better way of doing the old things, but of a perfect revolutionary way.

Stranger and stranger is verse 3, with its emphasis on the sudden appearance and disappearance of Melchizedek. Of course he was a real mortal with a date of birth and a day of death. Yet Scripture does not know of his parentage or credentials or successor. He remains poised as the perennial king-priest, a dim shadow of the one who is truly 'priest for ever'.

Our Jewish writer may employ strange exegesis to the modern Western mind, but he would have been well understood by his Hebrew readers, and the Spirit speaks through that medium to every age. Along with the unusual man comes that unusual moment described and explained in verses 4-10. All Jewish people held Abraham to be truly great as the pioneer father of the race. Yet he gave a tithe to Melchizedek and was blessed by him. By this act Abraham acknowledged the sovereignty of the shadowy king-priest. So, the argument continues, Abraham's descendants, including the levitical priesthood, bow before the one to whom Melchizedek points.

A very remarkable Saviour (7:11-28)

Melchizedek stands alone, this voice from the past, but Jesus is genuinely unique, and one of the great psalms underlines the difference. Psalm 110 is one of the most quoted Old Testament passages. Jesus himself speaks of his lordship as being corroborated here (Mark 12:35-37). Tucked away in that messianic psalm is a reintroduction of Melchizedek and his relationship to Jesus:

> For it is declared:
> "You are a priest for ever,
> in the order of Melchizedek"
> (7:17).

This unique promise of a priesthood that lasts for ever was necessary because then, as now, all religious ceremonies were imperfect and passing. The Old Testament law was always pointing forward to a day of fulfilment, not to a better way of doing the old things, but of a perfect revolutionary way. So Jesus would come not from the priestly tribe of Levi but the regal tribe of Judah, David's line, and he was predicted with a solemn divine oath ('The Lord has sworn ...', v. 21). God is saying loudly, 'Watch this space'.

The Jewish religious world was dominated by genealogy, just as our rootless Western society spares no expense and uses up much time to trace one's ancestry and find that elusive reality, 'roots'. The Old Testament tells the story of the succession of priests of varying worth. But good and bad alike, all suffered from the same weakness. They all died!

> We all depend upon human love in family and friendship, but inevitably there will be disappointments and frailty. This is different with him. What a friend we have in Jesus!

So, too, did Jesus, but, risen and ascended, he lives for ever and his ministry in heaven speaks not only of a completed work, but also of a continuing work: 'But because Jesus lives for ever, he has a permanent priesthood' (v. 24). The work of atonement is over and our heavenly status sure, but his work as high priest continues in intercession (v. 25—see also Rom. 8:34). Here is a unique priesthood which relegates Old Testament priesthood to history, and all modern attempts to revive it to dangerous irrelevance.

With verse 25, who wants more? Here is the promise of one who is able to save 'completely', 'to the end'. For assurance in the hour of doubt or testing, this verse ranks alongside John 13:1, with its promise of Jesus loving 'to the end' (NKJV). It speaks of absolute, complete, unending love. We all depend upon human love in family and friendship, but inevitably there will be disappointments and frailty. This is different with him. What a friend we have in Jesus!

Melchizedek's work is done, and he can now go back into the mists of history. We are left with this unique person, high priest and sacrifice all in one, all ancient prophecies fulfilled. In every way Jesus meets our needs. In his humanity, he understands us perfectly; in his sinless perfection, he can become the unique sacrifice for us. So in verse 27, the special words of this letter recur—'once for all'. To find a human counsellor who understands us is a difficult thing. For someone who can link that responsibility with an ability to meet our deepest need of forgiveness and hope there is only one candidate, and he offers himself to us, as well as to these Jewish converts, unreservedly.

For further study ▶

FOR FURTHER STUDY

1. Study again the Old Testament references in this chapter and think about the remarkable prophetic strain in Scripture.

2. What is Christ doing in heaven now (see Romans 8:34)? What dimension does this give to our Christian assurance?

TO THINK ABOUT AND DISCUSS

1. How should we respond to these truths about Jesus' unique role?

2. In what ways is the love of Jesus for his people like that between close family members and friends? In what ways is it different? How does knowledge of this love affect our daily lives? How should it affect our relationships? Our church life? Our walk with God?

7 Ancient and modern

(8:1-9:28)

As people age, there is always a tendency to glamorize the past. I remember a hymn book from my younger days with the title of this chapter. Memory suggests that the 'ancient' outnumbered the 'modern'. Fortunately, recent years have seen a very happy flowering of new Christian hymns and songs, and the wise pastor or music leader today will encourage a good blend.

When you remember the particular temptation of the Hebrew Christians to whom this letter was written, to go back to the old ways of the Jewish faith, you begin to understand the thrust of chapters 8 and 9, seen by the writer as the pivot of the book. Here he begins 'to crown the argument', introducing it with, 'The point of what we are saying is this ...' (v. 1a).

This section ends in 9:28 with the bold affirmation that

Christ's death was a 'once for all' event to deal with sins, and that his eventual return will be to bring the fullness of salvation, with the resurrection of the body, to those waiting for him. This follows on from the equally bold statement of the previous verse, that death has a one hundred per cent record—it happens to all of us once, and then there is the judgement. In one sweep of the pen all ideas of reincarnation are killed, in keeping with the overall thrust of Scripture. In such a solemn context, issues of 'eternal redemption', 'salvation' and 'inheritance' are at stake.

In our relationship (8:1-13)

These readers would have been very familiar with all the trappings of temple worship. These were not unimportant. In God's planning it was all a copy of what was to come (8:5). Back in history, Moses had built a tent for worship following the divine blueprint. It pointed to the urgent need for sacrifice because of sin and the promise of forgiveness through God's mercy and the shedding of blood. All this was the shadow coming from the cross, where the ultimate sacrifice would be made. Now we are transported into the real temple, the heavenly sanctuary (8:1-2).

In that sanctuary is Jesus seated in heaven, work done. He was never a priest in earthly terms, where the work was never finished, always needing to be repeated. His priesthood is 'superior' (v. 6) as he has made the way for a relationship which the old covenant could never bring about. Because of our failure to keep God's law, we could never achieve peace with God. Happily, God had other plans.

Now begins the longest New Testament quote from the

Old Testament, so important is its message which these Hebrew Christians were in danger of forgetting. It is introduced with the simple conviction that Jeremiah 31 is not just a prophetic word from a courageous, sensitive man longing for better things for his beloved nation. It is all that, but much more. So verse 8 introduces the quote as God speaking with an offer of a new covenant of promise to a people aware of failure and disobedience:

> The time is coming, declares the Lord,
> when I will make a new covenant
> with the house of Israel
> and with the house of Judah.
> It will not be like the covenant
> I made with their forefathers
> when I took them by the hand
> to lead them out of Egypt,
> because they did not remain faithful to my covenant,
> and I turned away from them,
> declares the Lord
> (8:8-9).

These words of Jeremiah came alive dramatically some six centuries later in a Jerusalem upper room when Jesus poured out wine and said: 'This cup is the new covenant in my blood' (1 Cor. 11:25). Through his foretold death on the cross, to which the Lord's Supper always points, all the offers of a new relationship are now available to be enjoyed personally, just as we take the cup and drink personally.

The first offer is of God's law in our hearts (v. 10). This links in with the promise of Ezekiel that God was in the

business of giving a new heart to his penitent, returning
people (Ezek. 36:26-27). Only an older generation today will
remember the day of the first physical heart transplants and
the wonder it engendered. Now it is a regular, if still skilful,
operation. The spiritual equivalent has been around for
centuries, but it is still a marvel, and one of its clearest proofs
is that now the recipient is given strength not to live just as he
or she likes, but to keep the unchanging demands of God's
law (see Rom. 8:3-4).

In this new relationship between God and his people,
which will have its full meaning only in heaven (Rev. 21:3),
there is now the wonderful reality of a personal knowledge of
God in terms of verse 11:

> No longer will a man teach his neighbour,
> or a man his brother, saying, 'Know the Lord',
> because they will all know me,
> from the least of them to the greatest.

This is not intellectual knowledge about God, but the
intimate knowledge that comes from a deep personal union,
of which marriage is the closest picture. Such a knowledge is
at the very heart of the Christian faith which dares to sing 'I
am his and he is mine'.[4]

In our ritual (9:1-10)

Ritual seems very unimportant to most Christians today, and
we are therefore relieved when we read 9:5b to discover that
the author has no time or space for further details on the
furniture of the Jerusalem temple. However, a little thought

reminds us that even the most informal worship has its rituals, even to the extent of always repeating the last line of the latest chorus!

The old sanctuary was full of symbolism, not least in its message that it alone could not meet the deepest needs of men and women (v. 9). From the days of the wilderness tabernacle the truth of God's holiness had been illustrated by the law of God; this was kept in the sacred ark and overshadowed by the atonement cover that spoke of God's way of bringing hope to people condemned by that law.

We ought to ensure that the buildings where we worship send out the right message, which includes awe as well as welcome. Supremely, our new 'sanctuaries' should speak of a work of salvation accomplished and available for all who respond in faith. So a church does not have an altar speaking of sacrifice repeated, but a Holy Table with a meal of fellowship offered by our

> We ought to ensure that the buildings where we worship send out the right message, which includes awe as well as welcome. Supremely, our new 'sanctuaries' should speak of a work of salvation accomplished and available for all who respond in faith. So a church does not have an altar speaking of sacrifice repeated, but a Holy Table with a meal of fellowship offered by our victorious High Priest to his redeemed family.

victorious High Priest to his redeemed family. How different from the solemn annual ritual of the Day of Atonement detailed in Leviticus 16, and mentioned here in verse 7.

In our redemption (9:11-28)

Some things must not change. The Christian faith cannot be written afresh to match the moods of every culture and age, nor must it ever forget its roots in the Old Testament. So the words of Hebrews 9:22 remain unalterable truth—there is no forgiveness without the shedding of blood. All the temple sacrifices proclaimed this loud, clear, and consistently. The cross of Calvary announced the perfect fulfilment of these, and the one common factor among all who enter heaven is that they have been cleansed through the blood of Christ (see Rev. 7:14).

> Some things must not change. The Christian faith cannot be written afresh to match the moods of every culture and age, nor must it ever forget its roots in the Old Testament.

For our generation the message is largely unacceptable, even repulsive. That is why Mel Gibson's explicit film 'The Passion of the Christ' caused such a stir, not least among liberal theologians. To the first readers of this letter the problem was different. Blood and sacrifice were common realities. Yet they needed to know that the transient sacrifices were now finished because the unique sacrifice had been made with eternal consequences.

The adjective 'eternal' has a double appearance here. It is

linked in 9:12 with redemption ('He did not enter by means of the blood of goats and calves; but he entered the Most Holy Place once for all by his own blood, having obtained eternal redemption') and in 9:15 with inheritance ('For this reason Christ is the mediator of a new covenant, that those who are called may receive the promised eternal inheritance'). It means much more than 'for ever and ever', although that is a glorious prospect in a world of change and apparent chance. Its primary note is of a new quality beyond all our earthly dreams. Yet it depends on a great event in the here and now, the death of Jesus outside Jerusalem's walls. Just as the beneficiaries of a will cannot inherit until a death occurs, so with the believer (9:16-17). What a death that was, and what great benefits we enjoy as a consequence!

For further study ▶

1. Jeremiah 31 is clearly pivotal in the Bible. What are the various elements of the 'new covenant' offered to us in Christ?

2. 'The life ... is in the blood' (Lev. 17:11). What does this statement really mean, and why is it so crucial?

TO THINK ABOUT AND DISCUSS

1. What 'rituals' do we have in our churches today? Do they send out the right message—that of Christ's finished work and God's offer of salvation in him? Or are there any that might detract from the message of the gospel?

2. How we can ensure the right balance between awe of God and boldness and intimacy with him in our worship services? Do the services in our church tend towards one extreme?

3. Are there ways in which we are sometimes guilty of 'toning down' the gospel message because we know others will not like to hear it? Why is it important not to miss things out, but to tell the whole of the gospel?

8 Revolution in worship

(10:1-18)

Christians are rarely seen as pioneers of revolution. Holding on to revealed truth creates an innate sense of conservatism. So Jeremiah urged his readers to 'stand at the crossroads and look; ask for the ancient paths' (Jer. 6:16).

Yet the truths of Hebrews 10:1-18 hide a remarkable revolution for Jewish Christians. After all the centuries, gone in one fell swoop were animal sacrifice, the historic priesthood, and temple regulations. Verses 2-3 suggest that this letter was written sometime before AD 70, with the Jerusalem temple activity still in full swing.

The revolution is one of theology, not the frantic attempt to keep relevant at all costs or to stir up apathetic worshippers, as so often are the feeble faithless desperation measures of our day. Calvary has changed everything. Through the unique sacrifice of Christ on the cross, believers have been set apart as holy people (v. 10) and because of the power of that event, they are being sanctified. Such believers are a revolution in themselves and need radical worship to match.

No entry (10:1-4)

That is the road sign that has been placed over pre-Christian worship, and the Temple prohibitions proclaimed it loud and clear. The difference between BC and AD was dramatic. Before Christ, all was in shadow awaiting the light of fulfilment. Sacrifices had to be repeated endlessly—'year after year' (v. 1) for the awesome ritual of the Day of Atonement; 'day after day' (v. 11) for the more homely regular temple sacrifices. It all demonstrated that nothing of lasting value had been effected. Sadly, some contemporary Christian worship has all the marks of this type of spiritual cul-de-sac. We keep coming, but we get nowhere.

The old way of worship had its own merit for its own times. It preached symbolically the very great sinfulness of sin and it majored on the shedding of blood as the divine answer. But there was no assurance of cleansing done, of forgiveness received. What was true before Christ is still true without Christ. These Hebrew believers, with so much to remind them of the old ways, needed to turn their minds afresh to gospel truths. A similar awakening had to come at the time of the Reformation, when Protestantism cut through much dead wood of Roman Catholic dogma in the rediscovery of New Testament teaching, and we dare never go back that way in a false concern for ecumenical reconciliation.

One way only (10:5-18)

Scripture is dominated by the person of Christ. Already we have noted the barrenness of the scene before Christ or without Christ. Now we are introduced to the glorious vista of what is ours through Christ and with Christ. There is even the daring assumption in verse 5 that the important quotation from Psalm 40 is from Christ himself. Link that with verse 15 and the assertion that the Holy Spirit is the author of this quote from Jeremiah 31, and you have a full-blown acknowledgement of the divine inspiration of Scripture.

Behind Psalm 40 is the great truth that God requires not some substitute offering, but our very lives: 'Then I said, "Here I am—it is written about me in the scroll—I have come to do your will, O God"' (v. 7; see also Rom. 12:1). In that spirit, Jesus offered his life to the Father. It was the principle which ever motivated him (John 4:34) and which he maintained at great cost all the way to Calvary. The story of his wrestling in prayer in the garden of Gethsemane is a vivid illustration of that cost—see Luke 22:42. For all in every age, including ours, who have been called to pay the ultimate price of allegiance to Jesus, here is the greatest place of encouragement. We are not alone. Over every call to obey against every instinct of comfort and peace is the phrase 'not my will but yours'.

The shadow of Christ's unique act on the cross should be seen across every part of Christian worship. If this were true, there would be a remarkable dynamic, with theological truth dominating the theme, balance and spirit of worship in its

> The cross is always at the centre, hence the rightness of our long-established logo and the folly of trying to reinvent symbols to seek to be relevant. Not surprisingly, in history the devil has often sought to attack the cross or tempt the church to find some other focus of attention. Is it not intriguing that one of the most evil regimes of the last century had the swastika, the broken cross, as its defiant symbol?

narrow sense of Sunday activity as well as in its wider sense of daily living. The boldness of prayer in verse 19 will be matched by the boldness of witness in verse 23. So, in contrast with the continuing work of the priest, faithful but unavailing, the present ministry of Christ in heaven will be the prevailing note.

In one sense, Christ's work is all done, and the ascension message is that God the Father has accepted his sacrifice on the cross. It is a pity that, with chronological accuracy, we keep Ascension Day on a Thursday, thus missing the prominence which the truth deserves. In Hebrews, the resurrection is mentioned only once, in the doxology of 13:20, whereas the ascension dominates the whole book. We are wise not to leave the story at Easter Day.

Salvation's story is all encapsulated in these verses, because in verse 13 there is the anticipation of the day when all of Christ's enemies will be finally defeated and he will return in triumph: 'Since that time he waits for his enemies to be made his footstool' (see also 1 Cor. 15: 25-27). All the tenses of salvation are present here, not least because verse 14 speaks of believers 'being made holy', a present, continuing work. In answer to the now rarely asked question, 'Are you saved?', we can correctly say 'I am ... I am being ... I shall be saved.'

The cross is always at the centre, hence the rightness of our long-established logo and the folly of trying to reinvent symbols to seek to be relevant. Not surprisingly, in history the devil has often sought to attack the cross or tempt the church to find some other focus of attention. Is it not intriguing that one of the most evil regimes of the last century had the swastika, the broken cross, as its defiant symbol?

At the foot of that cross Christian believers have been set apart in terms of verse 10 ('And by that will, we have been made holy through the sacrifice of the body of Jesus Christ once for all'), just as in baptism we may have been signed with the sign of the cross in commitment. Equally, through the same sacrifice of Jesus we are being transformed (v. 14). Here we have the assurance of sins forgiven, thus freeing us from the tyranny of guilt, and here we have the supreme incentive to live holy lives, remembering the cost of our deliverance.

For further study ▶

1. Think about the essential nature of the Reformation in the sixteenth century. Why was it so important? What Reformation principles are at stake in our churches today?

2. 'Inclusiveness' is an 'in' word for today's church. To what extent should the church be all-inclusive? Where should it be exclusive?

TO THINK ABOUT AND DISCUSS

1. What do we tend to think of when we call for a 'revolution' in worship? What are some of the measures churches today adopt? How far do these accord with what the writer to Hebrews is talking about here?

2. How do we use the symbol of the cross in our church life, in architecture and liturgy?

9 Resolution in witness

(10:19-39)

Hebrews 10:19 has one of the many 'therefore's of the New Testament epistles. This simple word marks an important transition and provokes a simple question: 'What is it there for?'

ere, as always, 'therefore' reminds us that creed should lead to conduct, belief to behaviour. Some believers major on orthodoxy of belief and others, sitting loose to doctrine, are keen to stress Christian action. What the Bible has joined together, let not the reader put asunder!

With that health warning goes another reminder that Scripture is always gloriously and sometimes challengingly balanced. Later in this chapter comes a paragraph of solemn warning and yet loving reassurance. The sense of urgency seems to be heightened by the reference to 'the Day approaching' in verse 25. This reference may have a double meaning, with one eye on the return of Christ, always just round the corner for the faithful, yet almost certainly with a more immediate reference—the imminent Fall of Jerusalem in AD 70, which Jesus anticipated in his teaching in Matthew 24.

Be encouraged (10:19-25)

This section starts in our life of worship, with all its rich meaning. This should be characterized by 'boldness' (or 'confidence'), a favourite word of the writer (see 4:16), and the very opposite of the timidity which normally marks our contemporary Christian. A reminder of the privilege we have in prayer and the cost involved in making the way possible in verses 19-20 should help us to overcome our natural reluctance and laziness in the sphere of prayer: 'We have confidence to enter the Most Holy Place by the blood of Jesus, by a new and living way opened for us through the curtain, that is, his body'.

> Boldness, however, is no excuse for acting presumptuously. An old Christian hymn proclaims that I may come 'just as I am', but never 'just as I like'.

Boldness, however, is no excuse for acting presumptuously. An old Christian hymn proclaims that I may come 'just as I am', but never 'just as I like'. Jesus told a story about a wedding feast to which people were invited from the highways and byways, and yet one man was thoroughly rejected because he refused to wear the offered accredited wedding garment (Matt. 22:11-13). So here in verse 22, there are certain conditions which must ever mark the sincere worshipper: 'Let us draw near to God with a sincere heart in full assurance of faith, having our hearts sprinkled to cleanse us from a guilty conscience and having our bodies washed with pure water.' Indeed, sincerity is at the very heart of it.

Christians must always look outwards as well as upwards, and with equal boldness. Here, too, there is need for sincerity. 'The hope we profess' (v. 23) not only bolsters the confidence of the believer, it also affects our witness in the world. In a society often characterized by hopelessness and despair, as reflected in popular songs and slogans, this witness is powerful. It all links with the faithfulness of God in keeping his promises, a strength to the believer and an offer to the seeker.

Nor are we in it alone. Strong language is used here. We are called to 'spur one another on towards love and good deeds' (v. 24). The verb means to 'provoke', and elsewhere in the New Testament it has a negative connotation. So Paul and Barnabas in Acts 15:39 had a 'sharp disagreement' over John Mark and his future; so in 1 Corinthians 13:5 love 'is not easily angered'; both these passages use our fellowship word! We are exhorted to cause a stir, but one which leads to love and Christian activity. Such stirring cannot be done from a distance.

Human nature changes little and the temptation to keep aloof from fellowship happened in the first century as much as in the twenty-first. From other writers we know what excuses were found for absenteeism from church attendance. There was ignorance of the truth about the importance of togetherness in the work of the gospel; there was a spirit of superiority believing that 'I do not need others'; there was a fear of being counted among a dubious crowd; there was that natural laziness, not wanting too demanding a commitment.

With one eye on the clock in world affairs ('all the more as you see the Day approaching'), we all need the mutual encouragement of verse 25, exemplified by Barnabas in Acts (his nickname means 'son of encouragement'). Whether befriending Paul after his conversion, speaking on behalf of John Mark in that famous confrontation with Paul, or seeing the grace of God at work in the young, somewhat revolutionary church in Antioch, Barnabas was always living up to his name. Churches today need a whole family of Barnabas-clones.

Be warned (10:26-31)

After all this encouragement comes a solemn word of warning. Verse 26 begins in the original with the simple word 'for', a reminder that Christian fellowship and witness is all the more necessary because of those who have gone back on their original faith and commitment. Again, nothing changes. But there should always be a health warning about a paragraph such as this: the writer does not have in mind those who temporarily fall away or lose their zeal. The person in this grim frame is the one who deliberately goes against the truth he or she once professed, or denies the faith he or she once believed and proclaimed.

There is almost an unholy trinity in verse 29 with reference to a denial of the deity of Christ, a despising of the message of the cross, and an insult to the Spirit of grace. False teachers of every age are in danger of these perilous tragedies and the doom is clearly spelt out. There can be nothing more serious than falling into the hands of the living God in his vengeance (v. 31). We do need to be aware of over-sensitive souls who are all too easily self-condemning, but we may not, however, ignore the danger and the doom these verses portray. Picking and choosing, in terms of which Scriptures we accept and which we reject, is a constant pitfall.

Be strengthened (10:32-39)

Like a good doctor, the writer has given a warning not primarily to frighten, but to remind the Hebrews of a better way of living. He has two weapons in his armoury. First, he calls them in verse 32 to 'remember', ever a good Christian exercise. It had become easy to forget the first zeal for the gospel in spite of persecution and prison. This forgetfulness can happen in individuals and in churches, and is often the by-product of more comfortable days. Just as wartime days can produce a new solidarity in the hour of danger, so tough days for the gospel can draw Christians together and nerve the arm; days of ease do the reverse.

The other weapon is his expression of confidence in his readers that they will, in fact, show resolve. He does that beautifully in verse 39 by putting himself in the equation, with one of those 'we' passages that make you walk tall. Testing days are coming; resolve is needed; but we move towards the day of the Lord's return and all its glory.

For further study ▶

FOR FURTHER STUDY

1. Watch Barnabas at work in Acts (4:36-7; 9:26-9; 11:22-6; 15:36-40). How can we be like him in our church situations?
2. Think through the implications of the unity and diversity of the body of Christ in 1 Corinthians 12:12-31 in the light of our contemporary church structures.

TO THINK ABOUT AND DISCUSS

1. In what ways can we be timid as Christians today? How do we need more 'boldness'? How does knowing how much Christ's sacrifice cost encourage us to be bold in our witness?
2. Where do we see hopelessness in our society today? What do we as Christians have to offer to people without hope? How can we reach such people with our message?
3. How does Satan sometimes tempt us to miss church services? Does he sometimes use legitimate concerns or responsibilities to keep us away from church? What dangers do we risk if we get into the habit of missing church? How does our local church suffer if we stay away?

10 Faith in action —Part 1

(11:1-22)

Hebrews 11 has become one of the best-known chapters in Scripture. The heroes and heroines of faith portrayed here make a stirring impact on readers in all generations.

Yet this passage may have been an afterthought, one of the special acts of Holy Spirit inspiration. To move from 10:39 to 12:1b is a smooth transition. On the other hand, these forty verses introduce us to great men and women, whose stories remain a challenge and encouragement to faith. We are not to think of this 'great cloud of witnesses' (12:1a) as watching from heaven and checking on their successors in the race. Rather, their lives are to be read and copied as we keep running.

There is a lovely balance in this chapter of the well known and the anonymous (vv. 35-38) between those who knew miraculous intervention on their behalf, and those who stood true and loyal even though their lives ended in martyrdom. The overall theme of the letter, with its concern not to turn back, has many echoes here, not least in verses 15-16. In the process of telling the stories we have this remarkable definition of 'faith', one of those religious words used often without much substance.

Essential faith (11:1-3)

There is no better definition of this elusive word than verse 1: 'Now faith is being sure of what we hope for and certain of what we do not see'. People often excuse themselves as not being able to believe, as if faith were a matter of genes. All human beings live by faith, not least in our technological age. What matters is WHERE we place our trust, and on what grounds. Faith is firstly trust in the future, moving into the realm of hope. The great Hebrew leaders in the Old Testament exhibited this in abundance, trusting God's promises, as did Abraham, the pioneer of journeying faith, or Jacob and Joseph in Egyptian exile, dying but still looking to the future Promised Land (vv. 21-22).

> People often excuse themselves as not being able to believe, as if faith were a matter of genes. All human beings live by faith, not least in our technological age.

Christians are always 'resident aliens' on earth, and those also for whom the spiritual dimension is real—'certain of what we do not see'. So Moses could stand unafraid before Pharaoh because he was more aware of the presence of the real King in his life (v. 27). It all follows from the truth of verse 3: since we live in a world created out of nothing, trusting the creator God who has not gone out of business.

Such faith changes our whole perspective in life. Just as a view from an aircraft diminishes the size of things on the ground, so an awareness of the reality of the eternal world makes molehills out of our current mountains (see 2 Cor. 4:17-18). That awareness comes from a confidence in God's Word. The recurring phrase in the story of creation in Genesis 1 is 'and God said'. By God's Word creation came into being and is still sustained (Ps. 33:6, 9). The Christian's trust is not in some vague spiritual reality, but in the truth of Scripture. 'Faith comes from hearing the message, and the message is heard through the word of Christ' (Rom. 10:17).

Embryonic faith (11:4-7)

Soon we shall be introduced to massive men of faith in Abraham and Moses, but first we have a glimpse into the shadowy world of 'the ancients'. Abel, Enoch and Noah are part of our human story. They tell us that effective living has always been 'by faith', a phrase with which each paragraph begins in this astounding chapter. It is the message of what God requires. The story of Cain and Abel is highlighted here. Abel's sacrifice was accepted not because it was animal rather than vegetable but because it stemmed from genuine trust, a matter of the heart and not just of ritual. The same theme would dominate later Hebrew prophets trying to bring spiritual reformation in days of dead religion. So the martyred Abel keeps on speaking to us.

With Enoch, faith is grasping hold of what God offers. There is a monotonous refrain in the genealogies of Genesis 5: however long these men listed there lived, it all ends with the chilling words 'and then he died.' In verse 24 comes the startling exception: 'Enoch walked with God; then he was no more, because God took him away'. The stranglehold of death had been broken in a glorious anticipation of the New Testament resurrection hope.

Like Enoch, Noah also walked with God (Gen. 6:9). His special contribution to the gallery of pioneers of faith was his implicit obedience to God's commands in spite of evidence to the contrary. His ark-building was dramatic proof of taking God at his word. His actions more than his words were a condemnation to a sinful, disobedient generation. In the process, his ark became a prototype of salvation through Christ alone, and is seen as such through New Testament eyes (Luke 17:26-27; 1 Peter 3:20-21; 2 Peter 2:5).

Enduring faith (11:8-22)

Abraham walks tall as the great historic example of faith in action. He has a unique place not only in Jewish, but also in salvation history; not only demonstrating the initial commitment, but also the continuing demands of the life of faith. For him, faith meant stepping out into the unknown, leaving behind a civilization of security which he knew well. Here is the essence of the great doctrine of justification by faith alone (Gen. 15:6).

Thus began a life of pilgrimage characterized by 'tent and altar'. The secular was transient; the spiritual abiding. He pitched his tent and built his altar. The only piece of real property Abraham had in the Promised Land was a burial place, a fitting testimony to a man who was always on the move and looking forward to the final city, home of all the faithful in every age. With this kind of pilgrim spirit, material possessions are never priority number one in heart and mind.

So in 13:14, we too have nothing 'enduring' here. In that same spirit we draw nearer to Jesus who died 'outside the camp' (13:12).

Some years ago, Christians used to sing a song which celebrated a God who specialized 'in things thought impossible', and Abraham could have given good supporting testimony. In his case (and Sarah's, of course), it was a fairly significant matter of producing a son in old age. The promise had been made and, with some hiccups, Abraham trusted the God of promise (v. 11). Not only was Isaac born in due course, but a whole succession of generations of people of faith in every age, including you and me. Understanding and responding to this truth could revolutionize the current crisis between Islam and Christianity!

> The only piece of real property Abraham had in the Promised Land was a burial place, a fitting testimony to a man who was always on the move and looking forward to the final city, home of all the faithful in every age. With this kind of pilgrim spirit, material possessions are never priority number one in heart and mind.

Yet the writer is addressing not politicians but ordinary Christians. In his age, and ours, there will be tests of faith in abundance. Such Jesus had promised (see John 16:33), but always in the context of final triumph. Significantly,

Abraham's supreme test was on a mountain top not far from where Calvary stood (vv. 17-19). There he offered back his son, a moving story where faith and love battled hard. In the event, Isaac was not sacrificed, but a ram took his place, another of those biblical signposts towards the cross. Never was a human being any nearer the heart of the God who did sacrifice his Son than Abraham on that day. The dramatic difference was that Abraham's knife was drawn back at the eleventh hour; God's knife went all the way. How can any Christian deny the uniqueness of that moment, and not live humbly yet courageously in the light of it!

FOR FURTHER STUDY

1. How can God's dealings with men and women in the early chapters of Genesis speak to our world?

2. How does the dramatic story in Genesis 22 anticipate the central work of Christ?

TO THINK ABOUT AND DISCUSS

1. What are the different things people mean when they talk about 'faith'? How does real, biblical faith differ from the popular idea of 'faith'?

2. Have you experienced times when your faith in God has been tested? What have you learnt from such experiences? Have these lessons helped you in subsequent times of difficulty?

3. How can we learn from this gallery of heroes and heroines?

11 Faith in action —Part 2

(11:23-40)

The life of faith has never been easy. The 'great cloud of witnesses' in this chapter does not consist merely of the well known, but also includes a kaleidoscope of unnamed heroes, some who saw the miraculous in their lives and some who refused to compromise, whatever the cost. Faith in action will always involve looking forward and keeping going.

Isaac, Jacob and Joseph are given brief coverage as they tell the same story of faith in action making the future become a present reality (vv. 20-22). Moses, however, dominates as one who is seen as the father of the Jewish nation. Often he was revered without a full understanding of the significance of his life and work. Stephen, who had preached in the same way in which this letter was written, had highlighted his rejection as being signal proof of his place as a forerunner of the Messiah (see Acts 7:35). In that sense Jesus, though infinitely greater, followed in his footsteps.

Follow your leader (11:23-31)

Loyalty to Christian leadership is a neglected virtue and is later emphasized in 13:7, 17. In the hour of testing, it can be tempting to move away from the courageous lead of men and women of God, and even so-called leaders can opt for security and peace at any price. Such was not the way of Moses, and his life here is given the full treatment.

Moses would grow up to be the man who chose God's way and paid the price. It all began well with the courageous faith of his parents (v. 23), a faith that defeated natural fear. It is hard to over-estimate the importance of godly parenting. Our society with its standards too often demeans the influence of a stable home. For that priority we must constantly work, pray and perhaps sacrifice. Moses' story in Exodus 2 contains some remarkable acts of providence so that he could be both a prince in Egypt and also one nurtured in the ways of the people of God. For our children we must long for something similar.

Then the hour came for Moses to make his choice as to where his future lay. Worldly wisdom would have pointed clearly in one direction, but the eye of faith saw that the Hebrew slave people were those with a greater future in the divine plan than all the intellect and power of Egypt: 'He chose to be mistreated along with the people of God rather than to enjoy the pleasures of sin for a short time. He regarded disgrace for the sake of Christ as of greater value than the treasures of Egypt, because he was looking ahead to his reward' (vv. 25-26). It is always thus. Sin offers more pleasure in the short term, but it has no lasting satisfaction to give. A church will ever seek to encourage its young people to make courageous choices and, in leaving the way of the world, offer a life to help change the world.

In Scripture, Jesus Christ is never far away, and here in verse 26, Moses' dramatic choice, which would involve sacrifice and suffering to bring rescue to others, is linked with Christ. In a similar way, in Luke 9:31 we read that on the Transfiguration mountain Moses and Jesus discussed his 'exodus'. Moses could certainly add expert testimony (compare with 1 Cor. 10:4). All roads in the Bible lead to and from Calvary.

> Faithful leaders are vital in every age, but they will be ineffective unless they are followed by people who trust God's Word. The story of the exodus and the very chequered march to the Promised Land would provide much illustration.

In that spirit of faith, Moses went into exile, and then later, a more mature leader, he confronted the might of Pharaoh, more aware of the danger of divine displeasure than of a despotic king's wrath. Faith and its exercise is always the perfect antidote to natural fear. In contemporary Christianity this lesson is being painfully learned in many parts of our world and could well be on our Western curriculum soon.

Faithful leaders are vital in every age, but they will be ineffective unless they are followed by people who trust God's Word. The story of the exodus and the very chequered march to the Promised Land would provide much illustration. To step into the waters of the Red Sea, confident of them parting and remaining so for all to reach the other side safely, was certainly faith in action (v. 29). There could be no trial run, no rehearsal to give confidence. Equally, the apparently absurd command to march round the walls of Jericho for seven days (v. 30) was a powerful demonstration of the effectiveness of God's promise made real through obedience. So the story of 'the prostitute Rahab' (v. 31), a most unlikely candidate for this chapter, becomes a vivid picture of faith proved by works more than words (see James 2:25).

Forward in faith (11:32-40)

Possible candidates for this portrait gallery of heroes and heroines of faith are so many that in verse 32 the writer has to apologize for some glaring omissions, and in the process uses the first person singular, giving us the one sure clue to his identity. He is indeed male!

All six mentioned in that verse had many frailties and failures. The God who could use a man like Samson is a God of great patience, a reminder that this is not the record of great people who deserve a medal, but of ordinary people made extraordinary by grace. So we move into the anonymous section with a glimpse into the book of Daniel, as an example of the courageous witness of those who faced lions and the furnace, coming through victoriously and providing an allegory of the story of Israel (vv. 33-34).

Here, however, is no triumphalism. Faithfulness sometimes leads to martyrdom, as in verse 37, and tradition makes Isaiah this victim of being sawn in two; all this detail is to nerve first-century Jewish Christians for inevitable hostility. Down the centuries by the Spirit it comes to twenty-first century Christians in the Western world facing the same growing enmity to the positive proclamation of our faith. It is not without significance that the prophets are very much included here, for persecution was the normal lot of these men with their unequivocal message.

Of these people great in faith it could be said that 'the world was not worthy of them' (v. 38), but they had the assurance that they were moving towards a greater goal, and now that hope has become a reality. Once more we are in the realm of 'something better' (v. 40). With that to rejoice in, to live and fight for, we should only look backward in order to press onward.

1. Study again 11:23-28. What can we learn about leadership from the example of Moses?

2. If the writer had been given more time, what might he have said about those mentioned in verse 32?

TO THINK ABOUT AND DISCUSS

1. What pressures do we see today which undermine stable family life? How can we fight against these pressures in our own lives?

2. What are the promises offered by the world which seek to pull us away from following Christ? How can we resist them? How can we encourage young people in our churches to be bold in faith and to persevere, rather than yielding to the temptations of the world?

3. How can we take the knowledge of our inheritance to come and use it to spur us on to be courageous and faithful in times of trial?

4. How can we encourage and support our church leaders and pastors? Are there ways in which we can make their task of leading us easier?

12 The discipline of love

(12:1-29)

There is almost a sports arena atmosphere about Hebrews 12 and its opening paragraph. An Ashes Test or a football Cup Final resembles, at least in part, the Roman amphitheatre and gladiatorial contest. But here is the crowned King Jesus in view instead of the Emperor Nero, and instead of a baying crowd of spectators there is 'such a great cloud of witnesses'. It is more of a race than a fight; a marathon race, in fact.

The witnesses are the heroes and heroines of the previous chapter and, changing the metaphor to more biblical terms, we are watching them for encouragement rather than them watching us in examination. The challenge is to keep going in faith and hope, with the faithfulness of Jesus at great cost as the supreme incentive. The race will not be won unless there is a willingness to 'run light' and be rid of sins and unhelpful ways that hinder progress.

The athlete will always be characterized by consistent discipline (see 1 Cor. 9:24-27). In the Christian race, this discipline will stem from a loving response to the gospel, and there will be forces to give that extra incentive to subdue the flesh and overcome laziness.

The Father at work (12:1-11)

These Hebrew Christians needed little reminder that they were in a life and death struggle. It makes a big difference in times of trial to remember the price the Saviour paid at Calvary: 'Consider him who endured such opposition from sinful men, so that you will not grow weary and lose heart.' He always warned his disciples that they would share his sufferings (John 15:18-21). Indeed, having learned that lesson, the early church even rejoiced in the fellowship of suffering (Acts 5:41).

A quote in verses 5-6 from Proverbs 3:11-12 underlines the truth that discipline stems from genuine love. In our age which knows all too little of discipline, not least in the home, the truth may be harder to grasp, but it remains a parental prerogative to apply discipline and a right punishment in order to mould the character of the child and equip him or her for life. The earthly father will be limited—hence the phrase 'as they thought best' in verse 10—but it is a responsibility to seek to follow the example of our heavenly Father and rescue the biblical connotation of fatherhood from a thousand misconceptions.

The goal of God's fatherly activity is 'that we may share in his holiness' (v. 10), and this will be a lifetime work. C. S.

Lewis, in his book 'The Problem of Pain', encapsulates it vividly. 'God whispers to us in our pleasures, speaks in our conscience, but shouts in our pain, it is his megaphone to rouse a deaf world'.5

The family at work (12:12-17)

> In an age when people are desperate to keep physically fit, and sometimes to succeed in sporting events, how strange that we are often so lax in our concern for the race of life. So Paul exhorted church elders to 'Take heed to yourselves and to all the flock' (Acts 20:28).

God's activity still demands a response from us. We are called in verse 14 to 'make every effort' and in verse 15 to 'see to it', and the verb used is the root of the word for a bishop. It speaks of oversight, with its reminder that Christians always have a responsibility for others.

Self-discipline is one of life's most demanding activities. Not surprisingly, the author resorts to athletic metaphors to hammer home his point. This is the theme of verses 12-13. We must watch that we do not trip up and thus disqualify ourselves from the race. In an age when people are desperate to keep physically fit, and sometimes to succeed in sporting events, how strange that we are often so lax in our concern for the race of life. So Paul exhorted church elders to 'Take heed to yourselves and to all the flock' (Acts 20:28, NKJV).

Then comes the call to act responsibly towards the rest of the fellowship (vv. 14-17). Anything which militates against holiness of life must be nipped in the bud. To strengthen his case, the writer uses a well-known Old Testament character and his sad story. Esau was a popular kind of person, more obviously attractive than devious brother Jacob, but he was godless in his sensuality and materialism, and missed the blessing of God in the process. The message is clear enough, even if there is doubt over the true rendering of verse 17.

Does the verse mean that Esau could not find any way to change his attitude even though he was deeply disturbed? Or does it mean that he could not change his father's decision, however much he wept? Where there is honest doubt we can hear the message from both interpretations. Either way, we must never trifle with God nor assume that we can turn on the right spiritual response at will. God is sovereign and he will not be mocked. Keeping a watchful eye on others is no excuse for prying or gossip, but we are our brother's keeper.

The future at work (12:18-29)

What we believe about our future inevitably affects how we react here and now. Hebrew Christians no longer lived in the Old Testament dispensation, centred on Mount Sinai, but in the New Testament era, centred on Mount Zion. This is a kingdom of joy, not of fear, and yet God has not changed and needs to be approached with reverence and awe. So this chapter will end with the reminder that 'our God is a consuming fire' (v. 29).

These believers knew all about the solemn picture in the book of Exodus describing Mount Sinai and the old covenant (vv. 18-21). However they were now part of 'the heavenly Jerusalem' (v. 22), one day to be revealed in all its splendour, but already a great spiritual reality in which Jew and Gentile can rejoice. The beauty of verses 22-24 should be a constant stimulus to the discipline of love in our lives: 'But you have come to Mount Zion, to the heavenly Jerusalem, the city of the living God. You have come to thousands upon thousands of angels in joyful assembly, to the church of the firstborn, whose names are written in heaven. You have come to God, the judge of all men, to the spirits of righteous men made perfect, to Jesus the mediator of a new covenant, and to the sprinkled blood that speaks a better word than the blood of Abel.' The glorious picture of heaven with its angelic host blends with the assurance of belonging not just to the church on earth with all its shortcomings, but also to heaven where are names are written. In that spirit, Jesus had exhorted his disciples, excited with signs of victory over demons, to be more thrilled with the knowledge of their heavenly inheritance (Luke 10:20). Experiences of blessing are often very transitory; but the promises of Scripture never change.

> The glorious picture of heaven with its angelic host blends with the assurance of belonging not just to the church on earth with all its shortcomings, but also to heaven where are names are written.

Our God is also a faithful judge (see Gen. 18:25), and he has promised a future place for those who have become righteous through faith in the atoning blood of his Son. In the Old Testament, the blood of murdered Abel called for vengeance; in the New Testament, the blood of the murdered Jesus promised reconciliation and forgiveness (v. 24). Here alone is our hope. In the cross of Christ alone we glory. The Westminster Shorter Catechism reminds us that 'the souls of believers are at their death made perfect in holiness and do immediately pass into glory, and their bodies, being still united to Christ, do rest in their graves till the resurrection.'

Assurance should never lead to complacency, and verses 25-29 remind us that we are in the hands of a sovereign, powerful God who shakes creation and history. In our technological age, tsunamis and hurricanes remind us of our pigmy frailty, and events of international significance drive us back to confidence in the God who controls all things, and yet is our loving Father.

For further study ▶

FOR FURTHER STUDY

1. Study 1 Corinthians 9:24-27. To what does Paul liken the Christian faith? How does he say we should live this life of faith? What does this mean practically for us as individuals and churches?

2. Study the characters of Esau and Jacob in Genesis 25-27. What lessons do they teach us?

TO THINK ABOUT AND DISCUSS

1. How can we keep a balance between watching out for one another, and not prying or interfering?

2. How is an earthly father a picture of our heavenly Father? What are the limitations of this picture?

3. How can we ensure that we are frequently remembering our eternal inheritance in heaven? What difference should the knowledge of this glorious future make to the way we live our lives now?

13 The demands of faith

(13:1-25)

'Only a short letter,' says the writer in 13:22. But by today's e-mail standards, a letter which takes one hour to read aloud seems painfully long!

But Hebrews is a letter with a difference. Even a 'word of exhortation' seems too humble a reflection on this mighty teaching document. Yet it is a letter with the usual intriguing personal references. In verses 18-19 there is a request for prayer for the writer (the first readers would probably have known his identity). He keeps the message going to the end. This last chapter is well worth opening up.

Doctrinal teaching is still around, with verses 9-16 hammering home the main theme of the letter. Not least are the urgent ethical implications of that theme in verses 1-6, with two paragraphs on the issue of loyalty to leadership, perhaps acute in this community, but never low on the agenda of any church life.

The final benediction has become well known in many liturgies. As well as containing the only specific reference to the resurrection of Jesus in this book, it also sums up well the book's theme and challenge. Here is a prayer significantly to 'the God of peace', always an expectation of dynamic activity rather than of quiet contemplation (see Rom. 16:20; Phil. 4:9; 1 Thes. 5:23). Faith in such a God will have a clear out-working, but also a promised in-working by the Jesus Christ portrayed in verse 8, one of the best-known verses of this or any book of the Bible and yet only properly understood in context.

Faith's out-working (13:1-19)

The phrase 'outside the camp' is used several times in verses 11-13 and is the translation of the word 'profane'. Christians are called to share in that experience of apparent rejection alongside Jesus, but there is first a challenge to walk the way of the faith within the camp, to give the Christian community a distinctive mark. If that was true in the first century, it has equally urgent implications for the twenty-first.

Love will be the hallmark of this community, seen in verse 1 as brotherly love leading to hospitality—very important in a world when travelling believers needed to find a welcoming spiritual home with good meals on the menu! Our global shrinking world has very pertinent parallels. Even more challenging is the willingness to stand alongside our persecuted brothers and sisters in Christ: 'Remember those in prison as if you were their fellow prisoners, and those who are mistreated as if you yourselves were suffering'. Already in 10:32-34 there has been the suggestion that this solidarity was being lost. All too easily, security and comfort win the day. We must never be allowed to forget the price many of our fellow-believers worldwide pay for following Jesus.

The spirit of charity must be linked to the spirit of purity. There should never be a battle between charity and chastity. So the priority of marital fidelity is spelt out unambiguously in verse 4: 'Marriage should be honoured by all, and the marriage bed kept pure, for God will judge the adulterer and all the sexually immoral'. The UK in this century is fast becoming a place where marriage is a minority relationship and cohabiting is accepted as the norm, even in some church circles. This letter, in tune with the rest of Scripture, could not be clearer. Compromise here will dim our witness catastrophically.

Not surprisingly, the challenge of money follows that of sex (in v. 5). These two powerful forces have destroyed Christian witness all too often. Viewed positively, they can be equally powerful tools for good. The New Testament has much to say about our use of money and the secret of being content (see Luke 12:15 and 1 Tim. 6:6-10). In our society consistency here within the Christian camp can be very effective.

Then there is the call for the spirit of sacrifice, seen in verse

> Love will be the hallmark of this community, seen in verse 1 as brotherly love leading to hospitality—very important in a world when travelling believers needed to find a welcoming spiritual home with good meals on the menu! Our global shrinking world has very pertinent parallels.

> Our writer cannot forget the dangerous influences from outside the camp which could mar the witness of the Christian community. False teachers, normally characterized by enslaving legalism, hover like birds of prey (v. 9). Only a strong grasp of the truth will defeat them, and the same principle applies to the challenge of liberalism today

15 in praise and worship which are to be a priority in time and enthusiasm. That must be balanced in the next verse by the challenge to be doing good and sharing with others. All is rounded off with the call to be obedient to our leaders, accepting their authority and encouraging them in their often lonely responsibility. This is the out-working in practical terms of Paul's challenge in Romans 12:1 to present our bodies as a living sacrifice, much more demanding than the animal sacrifices known to these Hebrew believers, but much more fulfilling.

Our writer cannot forget the dangerous influences from outside the camp which could mar the witness of the Christian community. False teachers, normally characterized by enslaving legalism, hover like birds of prey (v. 9). Only a strong grasp of the truth will defeat them, and the same principle applies to the challenge of liberalism today. So the reference to our 'altar' in verse 10 leads into a reminder of the uniqueness of Christ's sacrifice 'outside the camp', dying in the place of condemned criminals, bearing the penalty of our sin, becoming a curse for us. After that there can be no value in mere ritual, and any teaching which diminishes the primacy of the work of atonement at Calvary must be rigorously opposed.

Faith's in-working (13:20-25)

Part of the thrust of the benediction in verses 20-21 is that the God of peace may work in us. There will be no effective out-working if there is no continuing in-working. That can be linked with the best-known verse in this chapter, perhaps in the whole book, verse 8. Yet even this verse must be understood in context: 'Jesus Christ is the same yesterday and today and for ever' is not a text for calendars, to revive the spirit. It is a promise, and a challenge to let him work in and through us by his risen power.

This Jesus of unchanging reality links in with the revelation of God in Isaiah 48:12 and Revelation 1:17. God is not merely unchanging in his nature, but is active in past, present and future. So with Jesus Christ. The Christ of yesterday is portrayed not primarily in his loving, teaching ministry, vital though that was, but in the reality and significance of his death. Immediately after our key verse, the writer goes on to emphasize the centrality of Calvary, and the benediction bases its secure foundation on 'the blood of the eternal covenant' (v. 20).

The Christ of today, risen and ascended, is the whole theme of this letter, hence the emphasis in the benediction on the power of the historic victory over death symbolized in the empty tomb, and his subsequent ability to work in these

Hebrew believers in the here and now.

This great verse 8, encapsulating so much, is sometimes misread. There is no reference here to 'tomorrow', only 'for ever'. In the sense of the power of the ascended Lord and his intercessory representative ministry in heaven, there is no tomorrow. In the terms of 7:24-25, he 'always lives to intercede'. Because of that the benediction ends with attributing glory to Jesus 'for ever and ever'. We never know how many tomorrows we may have, nor what the next one will bring but, strengthened by the unchanging truths of this letter and the reality of God's grace mentioned in verse 25, we can face them with courage and with hope.

FOR FURTHER STUDY

1. Study the references to 'the God of peace' (Rom. 16:20; Phil. 4:9; 1 Thes. 5:23) and think about God's activity in our lives.

2. How does the closing benediction of Hebrews (13:20-21) stand as a testimony to the truth of the whole letter?

TO THINK ABOUT AND DISCUSS

1. How can we support our brothers and sisters in Christ around the world who are being persecuted for their faith? How can we make sure that we do not forget them?

2. How can we show more 'brotherly love' within our churches?

3. What should our attitude be to our money and possessions? The West is dominated by a materialistic, consumer society: what are the particular temptations Christians face in such a society?

Endotes

1 'See, amid the winter's snow', Edward Caswall, 1814-78.

2 'From heaven you came, helpless babe', Graham Kendrick, b. 1950.

3 'There were ninety and nine that safely lay', Elizabeth C. D. Clephane, 1868.

4 'Loved with everlasting love', George W. Robinson, 1838-77.

5 C. S. Lewis, *The Problem of Pain,* London, 1940, p. 81.